THIS BOOK IS DEDICATED TO MY
10,000 AND ONE
STUDENTS

ISBN: 978-0-578-59175-9
Copyright December 2019
Follow The History Tree Series at
www.historytreeseries.com

f @oldtreesrock   @history_tree   @historytrees

Text and illustrations copyright © 2019 by Tana Holmes Girasol Publishing, LLC

All rights reserved. No part of this publication may be reproduced, distributed, or transmitted in any form or by any means, including photocopying, recording, or other electronic mechanical methods, without the prior written permission of the publisher, except brief quotations embodied in reviews and certain other non-commercial uses permitted by copyright law.

THE HISTORY TREE SERIES

The History Tree Series books are designed for little people to learn history in a fun way, to appreciate old growth trees, and to interact with their grown-up reader for enriched content. Each page has easy to read words and concepts for the children, plus additional content for the adult reader (labeled as READER GUIDANCE) to add to the story as they see fit. Some historical stories have sad or violent elements. It will be up to the adult to choose how much to share, and at what age. Enjoy and get out and see some of these trees in person, they are all in existence today.

If trees could talk, what would they say?

Would they recall as they sway,
then tell about events where they grew?

...as they grew?

Starting as just a little acorn,
our tree reached for the sun
and watched the grazing longhorns.

Now it's a wise old History Tree at The Alamo.

If its leaves could whisper
the story of "The Shrine of Texas Liberty,"
what would it teach us about our history?

Reader Guidance: The Battle of the Alamo was not only one of the most important events in Texas history, but in the history of the United States. Several million visitors come to San Antonio each year to see the spot where a small band of Texians faced overwhelming odds for the cause of liberty. This event and the men and women who took part in it are too important to be forgotten. The story is a powerful learning tool and has sparked an interest in history for many young people and adults. The Alamo story offers great lessons for our children who are learning integrity and values.

The tree saw it all happen and could tell the story best, of Texians with true grit and no quit...

Reader Guidance: Today residents are simply known as Texans; however, the name for people living in pre-revolution Texas era was a matter of some confusion. The Telegraph and Texas Register from November 7, 1835, used multiple terms- Texans, Texonians, Texasians and Texicans, but it goes on to say: "We believe that, both by the Mexican and American residents of the country, the name commonly used is Texians." Texas residents of Mexican descent, many of whom predated their Anglo neighbors, were more accurately known by the Spanish word "Tejano".

Alamo Tree learned COURAGE from a man named David Crockett. "Davy," as the tree calls him, wore a 'coon skin cap and kept gunpowder in his pocket.

This famous frontiersman
and fighter in the 1812 War came to The Alamo from Tennessee.
His Congressman job wasn't fun anymore.
Texas made him the hero of lore.

Reader Guidance: In 1835, Crockett headed to Texas looking for ranch land. In January 1836 he joined the Texas Volunteers in their fight to hold The Alamo against the Mexican Army. Crockett died during the siege and capture of the fort by Mexican troops on March 6, 1836. His death at the Alamo made him even more famous than his politics did. Through newspaper accounts and other writings, some more fiction than fact, Crockett's legacy of skill, humor, and honesty grew.

Davy was a hunter, a soldier, a politician and a father. Sadly, he died at The Alamo leaving three sons and three daughters.

Alamo Tree's eyes filled with tears when remembering the
Love of the Dickinson Family.

Captain Almaron, Mamma Susanna, and their baby daughter Angelina lived near The Alamo Mission where the tree could see. The Captain fought among the Texians until he fell as a casualty.

General Santa Anna let young mother Susanna and her baby go when the battle was done. He wanted Susanna to tell Texas that the fighters were all gone.

Reader Guidance: Susanna Dickinson's eyewitness account of the battle's aftermath remains one of the most reliable for Alamo historians. She and baby daughter, Angelina, survived the 1836 siege and battle of the Alamo. Susanna was shot in the leg leaving the Alamo when Santa Anna sent her to Gonzalez TX on horseback to spread word of the Texian defeat to the Texas Colonists.

Colonel William Barret Travis leaned against the rough bark of The Tree. He hadn't known just how heavy the burden of leadership would be.

The Tree watched Colonel Travis send his brave "Victory or Death" letter, pleading for help for his Texian rebels. He wrote that The Mission was surrounded and couldn't last without aid on all levels.

Reader Guidance: The letter signed "Victory or Death" and dated February 24, 1836 has come to be known simply as "The Travis Letter". Travis' help arrived on March 8th, but Colonel Travis perished with all of his men at The Battle of The Alamo on March 6, 1836.

Teamwork
Alamo Tree saw all kinds of people fight together for independence and freedom.

But with so many of General Santa Anna's men out there, could they beat 'em? Mexican soldiers sealed off The Alamo. The Texians waited and waited but they just wouldn't go.

And General Santa Anna
wanted Travis and Crockett to let him be the boss,
but if they quit and went home, liberty was lost!

So, for 13 days the Texians in The Alamo didn't budge, but General Santa Anna still held a grudge.

Reader Guidance: After a 13-day siege, Mexican troops under President General Antonio López de Santa Anna invaded the Alamo Mission. He ordered 257 people killed. The only survivors were Susanna and Angelina Dickinson, a slave named Joe, a freed black man named John, Jim Bowie's nieces, Gertrudis and Juana Navarro Alsbury, Mrs. Alsbury's baby Alijo, Ana Esparza and her four children, Trinidad Saucedo, Petra Gonzalez, and Brigido Guerrero. All others were killed in the battle or executed after surrender.

He captured the Mission and its people. Alamo Tree wondered, would this stop the revolution growing under the steeple?

Santa Anna won the day, but he got his due at a place called San Jacinto... But that's a story for another History Tree. You should read that tale so you know!

So, visit The Alamo. Find the biggest old oak inside the walls.
Stand near and listen for the voice of Freedom as she calls.
"Remember the Alamo" was the start of it all.

ABOUT THE AUTHOR

Tana Holmes is an award-winning thirty-year, professional educator, a mom, and a nature lover. As an author, Mrs. Holmes' work is endorsed by parents, artists, teachers, and librarians who feel that the concept of an ancient tree story teller is creative, entertaining and engaging. As more volumes in the series debut, she anticipates an opportunity to reach children globally with their own local "celebritree" story teller. Visit her and the History Trees at www.historytreeseries.com. If you have enjoyed Alamo Tree, please leave a positive review at www.amazon.com. Tana Holmes lives in Katy, TX with her husband, Bryant, and two rescue dogs.

ABOUT THE ILLUSTRATOR

Mahfuja Selim is a veteran freelance illustrator who specializes in childrens books. Her whimsical style attracts authors from around the world to her combination of modern digital drawings and traditional hand illustrations. You can find her character creations and locations in magazines, educational publications, games, packaging, and children's stories. It is plain to see why children love her work!

www.ingramcontent.com/pod-product-compliance
Lightning Source LLC
Chambersburg PA
CBHW081238080526
44587CB00022B/3986